to **T**... **Y**our **Connection**

FREE RESOURCES

Harvest Prayer Ministries, the parent
ministry of *Prayer Connect* and PrayerShop
Publishing, has multiple free helps that
can encourage you in your daily prayer life.
Here are some we invite you to check out:

Connection— a daily devotional on prayer that
includes some inspirational thoughts and several
Scripture-based prayer points. This can be emailed
or RSS-fed to you each day. View it, or sign-up at
harvestprayer.com/connection.

Scripture-Prayer— a daily passage of Scripture
to read and then prayer points to pray about, using
the passage. Designed to encourage you to practice
praying Scripture regularly. It also can be emailed
or RSS-fed to you each day. View it or sign up at
prayerconnect/blogs/scripture-prayer.

Prayer Guides — prayerconnect.net has a
section of free prayer guides on various subjects.
You are free to copy and use them in your prayer
times or in your group. They are all Scripture-based
prayer points or prayers. You will find them at
prayerconnect.net/resources/prayer-guides.

HARVEST PRAYER MINISTRIES

Websites:

We encourage you to check out our ministry websites. Each has prayer resources that can help deepen your prayer connection with God or help you grow prayer in your church.

harvestprayer.com	**prayerleader.com**
prayerconnect.net	**prayershop.org**
prayertoday.org	**greatercalling.org**
40daysofprayer.net	**strategicpi.org**
ministrytoday.org	**prayerretreat.net**

Like us on Facebook at
facebook.com/harvestprayer, facebook.com/ prayerconnect, or **facebook.com/prayerretreat**

LIVING

IN THE

UPPER ROOM

Permeate Your Church with a Culture of Prayer

COMPILED BY PRAYER CONNECT

PRAYERSHOP
PUBLISHING

Terre Haute, Indiana

This product represents the theme section of issue 10 of *Prayer Connect* magazine. Because the message of this theme is so crucial to the health and growth of a congregation, we offer it in this smaller, booklet format, as a way for churches to put it inexpensively in the hands of their leaders. Go to prayershop.org to see multiple copy discounts that are available.

PrayerShop Publishing is the publishing arm of Harvest Prayer Ministries and the Church Prayer Leaders Network. Harvest Prayer Ministries exists to equip the local church to become a house of prayer for all nations, releasing God's power for revival and finishing the task of world evangelization. Its online prayer store, www.prayershop. org, has more than 600 prayer resources available for purchase.

Contents

INTRODUCTION

I'm not sure I can adequately describe Joe. This very elderly, stooped-over Jewish man was rejected by his family when he became a follower of Jesus Christ. He was a bit quirky and had very few possessions. In fact, everything he owned fit into a suitcase. When Joe needed a ride, he would call and say he "needed a little fellowship." That meant you were to pick him up, take him to church, and then perhaps buy lunch for him on the way home.

My greatest appreciation for Joe came during times of prayer with him. He never missed a prayer gathering, and, in private, he prayed through the church directory every week, name by name.

I don't remember how I joined a little prayer

group with Joe and two other friends. But for a season, we prayed in what we called "the upper room." It was a tiny storage closet above the baptistery. We had to climb very steep stairs to get there and then duck to avoid hitting our heads once we were in the room. Getting Joe up there always presented a challenge, but if it was a prayer time—nothing could deter him!

In that upper room, we prayed for the church. We prayed for the salvation of the lost. We prayed about broken families. We asked the Spirit to do a fresh work in our congregation. Perhaps we were repeating some of the same prayers of the early believers in the original upper room.

Obviously it was not the room itself that made this prayer time special. It was because four people had something in common—we longed for Jesus to be powerfully manifested in our lives, church, and nation. Now I can look back and understand that praying with Joe, in all his quirkiness, was a privilege because Joe was completely devoted to his Lord. Joe's life was permeated with prayer. It was simply what he did, day after day, without fail.

Back to the Upper Room

Now, several years later, I believe God is awakening His Church to our desperate need to "live in the upper room." He is calling us to return to the same devotion to prayer that the early believers lived out. It is time again to assertively incorporate prayer into the very culture of the local church.

A *culture* can be described as the particular behaviors and characteristics that define a people group in a place or time. If your church is marked by a culture of prayer, it means that prayer—like breathing—is a natural and rhythmic necessity. You are known for your prayer lives. Your entire church embraces the mindset that it simply cannot survive if prayer is not foremost.

In this issue you will read from Fred Hartley about upper-room, God-encountering prayer as the launching pad for all ministry. Fred Leonard lists ten ways your church can move toward becoming a house of prayer. And you will gain insight from several pastors about how their churches have wrestled with creating cultures of prayer.

As it turned out, I missed Joe's funeral because

we had a Minnesota snowstorm that day. But I so wanted to see the many people who were touched in some way by Joe's prayer life. I had heard that he knew people all over the city. I'm not surprised. A praying man—and a praying church—always have great impact for the Kingdom of God.

—Carol Madison, editor, *Prayer Connect*

By Fred Hartley

FROM THE UPPER ROOM TO THE NATIONS

The church in Antioch may be separated from my congregation in Atlanta by 2,000 years and 6,400 miles, but we have much in common.

- We are both multi-ethnic.
- We both minister to the presence of Christ through worship—this is our primary assignment, and we know it!
- We are both missionally focused—to thrust world-impacting believers off the launching pad of prayer.

Twenty-five years ago the membership of Lilburn Alliance Church in Metro Atlanta was 99 percent white and English speaking. Today our congregation is made up of people who were born in 54 different nations of the world. We have hosted seven different cross-cultural congregations with whom we are ministry partners—Vietnamese, Spanish, Spanish second generation, Eritrean, Asian-Indian, French-African, and Chinese. Our Vietnamese congregation has planted seven other congregations around Atlanta, and has led more than 1,000 Vietnamese to faith in Jesus Christ.

None of this would have happened without devoting ourselves to Christ-encountering prayer. We follow the upper room model of ministry taught by Christ, demonstrated throughout the early Church and most vividly exemplified in Antioch.

The church in Antioch (see Acts 13:1–3 and Acts 11:19–29) was entirely multi-ethnic: Barnabas from the Mediterranean Island of Crete; Simon from Africa; Lucius, a Greek; Manaen, an associate of Herod the tetrarch, and Saul, a full-blood, pedigree Jew!

The eclectic believers all devoted themselves to ministering to the manifest presence of Christ by staying focused in their worship. They fasted. They hungered more for a move of God than for food.

As they knelt on the launching pad of prayer, the Holy Spirit spoke and said to the apostolic-prophets in their prayer-filled, God-encountering gathering: "Set apart for me Barnabas and Saul for the work to which I have called them."

They not only built a launching pad of prayer, they had ignition and lift off!

Guiding Principles

Before I tell our story of how God built a launch-ing pad in Atlanta, we need to understand several guiding principles.

- When Jesus built His church, He built a praying church. *What kind of church are you building?*
- When Jesus made disciples, He made praying disciples. *What kind of disciples are you making?*
- The size (scope) of your ministry is deter-mined by the size of your prayer life.
- The size of your church's prayer life is revealed by the size of the answers to prayer. *What are you asking God for?*

The Cape Kennedy Space Center on Florida's east coast built a most remarkable launching pad for the Space Shuttle—Pad 39. It was built to withstand more thrust than any other—36,000 pounds of thrust per square inch. Built of solid, poured concrete, it is 390 feet long, 345 feet wide, and an impressive 48 feet thick!

Jesus said, "Ask the Lord of the harvest, therefore, to send out [thrust forth] workers into his harvest field" (Matt. 9:38, bracketed material added).

If we want *thrust*, we need a launching pad—a sizable launching pad. As Rick Warren often says, "The significance of your church is not determined by your seating capacity but by your sending capacity." Sending capacity is determined by the thrust of the Holy Spirit. In order to sustain Holy Spirit thrust, we need a substantial launching pad of prayer.

Upper Room: The Crown Jewel

It was no mere coincidence that the only thing Jesus built while on earth was the upper room full of praying disciples. The upper room was the highest accomplishment of Jesus' discipleship ministry—

the crown jewel. The tragedy of the modern church is that Jesus' highest accomplishment has become our flagrant omission.

An upper room or *huperoon* in Greek (Acts 1:13) was common in the Middle East in Jesus' time. People gathered in the flat, open space on the rooftop of the square buildings for conversation—to sip tea, tell stories, welcome out-of-town guests, or unwind at the end of the day. For Jesus and His disciples the upper room provided a meeting place where they could talk, pray, plan, and eat together.

In one such upper room, Jesus broke bread, served the disciples the Passover meal, and washed their feet. Before He ascended into heaven, while gathered with them on the Mount of Olives, Jesus "gave them this command: 'Do not leave Jerusalem, but wait for the gift my Father promised, which you have heard me speak about'" (Acts 1:4). The word *command*, used in the military, is the strongest word in the Greek language for *decree*. So Jesus put them under strictest orders.

Obviously, 40 days earlier, when Jesus was begging them in the Garden of Gethsemane to pray with Him one hour, His disciples were not yet upper-room disciples. But now they were fully engaged. Something had changed. No sooner does Jesus bodily ascend into heaven, right before their eyes, than they demonstrate that transformation: "Then they returned to Jerusalem from the hill called the Mount of Olives, a Sabbath day's walk from the city. When they arrived, they went upstairs to the room [*huperoon*] where they were staying" (Acts 1:12–13).

The same disciples, who before couldn't pray one hour, now could pray the better part of 240 hours—ten straight days! Into that upper room He had led His disciples. Into that room He had poured out His Spirit. Out from that room He had thrust forth His empowered disciples. Out from that room He carried out His mission on earth.

In a matter of hours the early Church grew from 120 to 3,120. That kind of church growth would be impressive anywhere, but this happened in Jerusalem!

We, as a local church in Metro Atlanta, realized that this pattern of upper-room, God-encountering, launching-pad-building prayer is a prototype that continues through New Testament life. The initial upper room in Jerusalem was by no means the only upper room in the Book of Acts.

- Peter and John were on their way to an upper-room encounter with Christ when they met a lame man (Acts 3).
- The early Church had an upper-room, earth-shaking, prayer encounter with God (Acts 4).
- The apostles appointed deacons so they could remain devoted to upper-room prayer (Acts 6:4).
- Paul had an upper-room encounter with Ananias (Acts 9).
- Peter had an upper-room encounter with God (Acts 10).

The church in Antioch certainly built an upper room that launched the first mission team of Paul and Barnabas (Acts 13). In fact, every church Paul planted became an upper room. And when Paul launched a new mission trip, he was sent from the launching pad in Antioch.

An Upper Room in Every Church

When Lilburn Alliance Church saw this upper-room, God-encountering, launching-pad-of-prayer pattern, we realized we needed an upper room. We asked God for His blueprint and began a central, all-church prayer gathering known as the RIVER.

What makes an upper-room prayer gathering unique?

The primary focus of an upper-room prayer gathering has one ultimate purpose—to minister to the manifest presence of Christ. Just as in Antioch they were worshipping the Lord when God gave them their mission, so every upper-room prayer gathering has one agenda—to minister to the Lord with our prayer and worship. Until we understand that our first assignment is to minister to the manifest presence of Christ, God will not give us our second assignment.

It was in the RIVER one night that God put a burden on our hearts for the neighborhoods, apartment complexes, and subdivisions immediately adjacent to our church property. I saw a picture of myself going door to door, introducing myself and saying to the people, "I would like to pray for you—what would you like Jesus to do for you?"

This struck a chord with our whole church family. Since then, we have visited 5,000 homes around our church campus. At our Wednesday night AWANA kids clubs, more than half of the children are from the neighborhoods around our church. Muslim, Buddhist, and Hindu parents bring their children to our church. It looks like a meeting of the United Nations each week.

Now when I walk the neighborhoods around our church, most of the people recognize me, smile big, and many thank me for all our church is doing for the community.

During the past 25 years, we have seen more than 3,000 people come to faith in Christ through the personal witness and ministries of our people. I wish I could say they all became members of our church, but they have not. The greatest reward, however, is the knowledge that we will all be gathered before God's throne one day in united worship.

The Upper Room Today

The upper room is the closest place to heaven on earth. Just think about it. Jesus went from the throne room to earth to build the upper room. Before leaving earth He told the disciples to go to the upper room so that He could ascend back to the throne room. From the throne room through the upper room, He would then carry out His ministry on earth. This is the New Testament upper-room pattern.

In the first century the upper room was on the rooftop. For us the upper room can be in a basement, a chapel, or the back porch. The upper room does not need to be "upper" in location, but it needs to be upper in *priority* and upper in *prominence*. Upper-room, God-encountering prayer is the launching pad and lifeline of every church ministry and activity. Everything else is wood, hay, and stubble (1 Cor. 3:12–15).

Recently, when I preached a new message on the upper room to our people, a woman ministry leader came to me in tears and said, "Pastor Fred, that message described to a *T* what our women's meetings are like every Tuesday morning. Thank you for pointing us to keep first things first."

Though 6,400 miles separate my church in Atlanta from the church in Antioch, we share the same DNA. The same missional thrust that God created in Antioch, He is creating today in Atlanta some 2,000 years later. It is all coming out of a culture of prayer. We take seriously the words of Jesus, "Ask the Lord of the harvest, therefore, to send out workers into his harvest field" (Matt. 9:38).

Our mission is to reach a lost world through a revived church. A lukewarm church will never get the job done. My congregation in Atlanta wants to be part of reaching the remaining unreached people on earth. For this reason we take seriously our call to build a Christ-encountering, upper-room, launching pad of prayer.

FRED HARTLEY is lead pastor of Lilburn Alliance Church in Metro Atlanta, GA, where he and his wife Sherry have served since 1988. Fred is also president of the College of Prayer International with 119 campuses worldwide, serving more than 30,000 students. He has authored 19 books, including *Everything by Prayer, Prayer on Fire,* and his new book, *God on Fire (*available from *prayershop.org*).

By Fred Hartley

HOW TO BUILD A PRAYER CULTURE FOR A MISSIONAL CHURCH

While the Holy Spirit will show you the unique pattern for *your* particular congregation to become a house of prayer for all nations, here are some keys we have discovered in Atlanta and around the world.

1. The pastor sets the tempo. Jesus made praying disciples (Acts 1:4). John the Baptist made praying disciples (Luke 11:1). We, as pastors and leaders of our people, are the ones who make praying disciples. We dare not delegate prayer discipleship to anyone else.

2. Bring others with you. Just as Jesus, John the Baptist, and the Apostle Paul brought praying people along with them, we want to invite rising leaders to pray with us. The best way to learn to pray is with people who know how.

3. Build a prayer shield. A prayer shield is a group of personal intercessors who are recruited to consistently pray for the pastor(s)—prayers for God to protect them from the plots of the evil one and to empower them for service. I now have more than 400 people around the world who are committed to praying for me on a daily, or at least regular, basis.

4. Appoint a prayer team and a team leader. The prayer team in my local church is a powerhouse. They not only facilitate pre-service prayer—filling the room with the presence of God before our worship celebrations—they mobilize prayer throughout our church family.

5. Every meeting is a prayer meeting. We find that a prayer meeting breaks out more often than not in gatherings such as small groups, Sunday school classes, women's meetings, elders' meetings, and business meetings. We follow the pattern, *"everything by prayer"* (Phil 4:6).

6. Call for seasons of fasting. We call for fasts

through the year—seven days, 21 days, or 40 days. During these times of accelerated spiritual growth, we see dramatic answers to specific prayers.

7. Give invitations to meet God. In the middle of Sunday worship we call people to come to "The Garden of Prayer" at the front of the auditorium to meet God. We've discovered that church is not a place to hide from God; it's a place to meet God. People bring their highs and lows, their challenges and their blessings. Some weeks 50 or more people flood to the front and encounter God.

8. Emphasize mid-week prayer. Our mid-week corporate meeting is called the RIVER, a worship-based prayer gathering. We assemble chairs in concentric circles, which puts the focus on Christ and keeps us close enough to hear each other pray. It also gives opportunity to call people with needs into the middle of the circle so we can pray over them.

9. Ask for the nations. The size of our prayer life is revealed by the size of our answers to prayer. Therefore, we ask for the nations. What bigger thing can we ask for than the nations? When we began asking God for the nations, He began to expand our territory. We now have 54 nations worshipping together under one roof. "Ask of me, and I will make the nations your inheritance" (Ps. 2:8). God wants to take us all from the upper room to the nations.

—Fred Hartley

By Fred Leonard

"On Ramps" to God's Presence

I love the picture in Revelation 4 of John entering into the throne room and the presence of God. When he comes in, he finds himself in a scene of incredible, loud, radical worship of the Lord God on His throne.

When I pray, I picture myself entering the throne room of God through the open door in heaven. I can come in only because of the gospel of Jesus Christ, God's only Son, who died for me and paid the penalty for my sin. I am covered in the blood of Jesus.

As I enter in, in my mind I picture Jesus looking at me as one for whom He died. I picture the angels and 24 elders and the four living beings listening as I worship and present my requests to God—my act of prayer. It is an honor and privilege to enter into His presence through prayer.

With this reality, wouldn't it make sense that everyone would want to rush in and talk with God?

Sadly, this is often not the case. Some people can hardly pray privately, much less corporately. Our prayer meetings are not overflowing with people crying out to God. In fact prayer is one of the most difficult ministries to lead in the church.

Living in the Tension

One reason this ministry is difficult to lead is that followers of Christ live with the tension of God's Kingdom already here among us—and not yet fully realized. In other words, we still sin and rebel against God's rule in our lives. When we are not walking in submission to God's leadership, we are resisting the Holy Spirit. Unless we repent, we cannot be in right relationship with God, and we won't long to be praying and worshiping in the throne room.

Furthermore, if we are living in unforgiveness,

our broken relationship with God keeps us from entering the throne room—and we certainly don't want to enter with those who have hurt us! You can still teach Sunday school or be an usher or greeter while you are living in rebellion (though you shouldn't be), but rebellion will greatly hinder your prayer life.

Although discipling a church in prayer is difficult, we don't give up. We know the heart of God is to communicate with us. And—with determination and vision—we want to lead the church into this truth.

Here is our top ten list of ways a church can become a house of prayer for all nations:

10. Develop a strategic plan—or nothing will change.

To grow in prayer, be honest about your church's current status as a house of prayer. Take a look at what is working. Be willing to keep changing. And work to develop a strategic plan that will move you toward your goal. Without an honest evaluation of your current reality and a plan that looks toward the vision God has given you for your future, nothing will change.

9. Offer many "on ramps" at different speeds to help people begin praying.

Developing a prayer culture in our churches requires talking about prayer at all levels. This means providing many different on ramps for people to learn to pray personally and corporately. At our church people can grow in prayer by spending time alone in the prayer room—learning to pray for lost people or using the various prayer prompts we make available. This way they can practice prayer skills privately and then use them in a corporate setting.

Our corporate on ramps include a weekly missions prayer gathering, pre-service prayer, prayer during one of our services, or serving as a "prayer usher" (praying with people to help usher them into a fresh experience of Christ's presence). Each of our ministries (such as youth, recovery, and worship), also offers a pre-meeting prayer opportunity.

Another on ramp is our strategic teaching on prayer. We teach and encourage spiritual disciplines, offering a monthly prayer workshop and a "Love to Pray" study once a year, using prayer book studies through our prayer meetings. Our church is also committed to hosting prayer conferences.

To be a healthy, praying church, prayer should saturate everything. Beyond the teaching opportunities, we also encourage times of church-wide prayer. For example, we hold an Ash Wednesday service to begin the Lenten season of 40 days of prayer and fasting. Each year we have a month of special church-wide prayer for revival. We join with other churches and host the Global Day of Prayer, the National Day of Prayer, and city-wide prayer events. We participate in and help lead weekly prayer meetings for pastors. The list continues on with many prayer initiatives.

Prayer is not a ministry we do; it has become *who we are.*

8. Make sure the prayer meeting is awesome!

When a prayer meeting is boring, poorly led, and people- or need-centered, people won't likely keep coming. Our church offers workshops for our prayer leaders, teaching them how to lead corporate prayer. Our prayer meetings are characterized by four L's: Lively, Learning, Loving, and well-Led.

When people leave a well-led, God-centered, Kingdom-focused prayer meeting, they will know they have met with God. And they will appreciate even more their love relationship with Him.

7. Weave prayer throughout the fabric of everything you do. Keep learning and trying new things.

Prayer must be at the core of a pastor and prayer leader's life and be woven into the fabric of the church. We don't "silo" prayer into a separate ministry. We are a house of prayer that includes every "room" of the church. Prayer remains at the top of our list in everything we do. We may not get through all the business in every meeting, but you can be sure we have prayed. We might restructure our weekend services for a special event, but we will not disrupt our prayer ushers' ability to minister to people during the service, and we won't eliminate a prayer response at the end. Prayer is never simply an add-on.

It is also important to push the prayer envelope and try new things. We have offered prophecy training and now have prophecy appointments after the Sunday morning service every few months. We have healing services on Sundays, too. It's good to offer these things during the week, as well, but we find that when we offer them on the weekend, God opens doors for a fresh, forward movement in prayer. Experiencing the blessing of Spirit-led corporate prayer encourages people to discover that reality in their own lives.

6. Find the right leader for your prayer ministry. Appoint a teacher who is passionate about prayer and joyfully submitted to pastoral leadership.

It is crucial to have an equipper/teacher who has a heart for prayer and can release people into the ministry of prayer. This person, who needs to have learned through experience and struggles, also needs to have the gifting and ability to expand the ministry by training others.

Furthermore, he or she must be someone who is praying in support of the pastoral direction of the church. The pastor has God's authority to lead, and the prayer leader must support the pastor in prayer, words, and actions. Those in the prayer ministry should never pray against the pastor or work to change the leadership. Such actions cause division, disunity, offense, and bitterness—and they are an open door to the work of the devil. The prayer leader needs to be the greatest supporter and encourager of the pastor and of the vision the Lord has given to the leaders.

5. Train prayer ushers to minister to others.

We train people to usher others into the presence of Jesus and to minister to them through prayer. One of the greatest mistakes some churches make is to assume that people know how to pray, even if no one has taught them. What happens when a prayer usher meets a person in a prayer encounter and discovers the person needs to repent or surrender—or needs to experience healing or deliverance? Do your prayer leaders know what to do? Training a group of prayer ushers who pray under the empowerment of the Holy Spirit is a crucial part of church life.

4. Make prayer training the foundation of discipleship.

Some churches struggle in the area of discipleship as much as they struggle in evangelism. It is a challenge to see people experience both salvation and the transformation of "becoming like Jesus." We can track evangelism, but how do we track discipleship? I believe the best way is through prayer training.

We have created a prayer training class that encompasses much of what we need to know to walk with Jesus. We train people how to pray for such areas as evangelism, the empowerment of the Holy Spirit, forgiveness, using spiritual gifts, prophecy, listening prayer, healing, repentance, surrender, and freedom from sexual sins. As they pray through these components in their own lives, they learn to pray with others as well. They're intentionally being discipled to be like Jesus.

3. Remember that prayer always leads to evangelism.

When prayer is moving as it should, it will always lead to God's heart for the lost. Prayer does not become an end in itself but instead always leads to evangelism. Prayer for God's glory is the goal. And we know God receives more and more glory when people come to know Jesus as their Savior (2 Cor. 4:15).

Prayer has to move us to care for, reach out to, and love the lost. Prayer is not self-serving. In fact, it should be listed under the gift of helps. There is no way we can help others more than to pray for them.

2. Encourage the pastor to set the table and invite people to the banquet.

It is impossible for the church to move forward into prayer if the pastor is not on board and leading the staff and church in prayer. The pastor has to be championing prayer, attending prayer meetings, and spending time in the prayer room if he or she is to lead others.

Furthermore, as the pastor is leading and encouraging prayer, the staff and leadership also need to be on board—as people who pray, serve as prayer ushers, attend prayer events, pray in the prayer room, and participate in a prayer group each week. It is impossible to call people to do what we are not doing ourselves.

1. Pray and ask God to pour out His Holy Spirit.

The number one key to becoming a house of prayer for all nations is to be always praying and asking God to pour out His Holy Spirit upon you and to fill your church with His presence. Apart from the empowerment of the Holy Spirit, we will never see that vision become a reality. In order for a movement of prayer to take place, we need to intercede for our churches, asking God for the filling of the Spirit.

This is not a program or a strategy. It is a miracle of God to bring your church into His presence. In this way, your church will bring glory to His name.

FRED LEONARD is the lead pastor of Mountain View Community Church in Fresno, CA. His wife Esther is the prayer ministry leader of the church.

By *Dennis Fuqua*

SIGNS OF A CULTURE OF PRAYER

How do you measure the effectiveness of a culture of prayer in your church? Here are some signs that should be present:

1. "Here and now" prayer, rather than "later and somewhere else" prayer. When someone is asked to pray about a specific request, the norm is to pray right "here and now" rather than the request being put on a list and prayed for at another time when the person is not there.

2. There are a variety of prayer ministries, but the bottom-line goal is that each individual is being encouraged to be "devoted to prayer."

3. Leaders regularly describe and demonstrate their commitment to both personal and corporate prayer. This can happen in a passing reference as they preach or teach, or it could be more intentional. Also, they attend and invite others to be a part of any corporate prayer times.

4. Corporate prayer is a regular part of the weekend services. This can happen in many ways: small groups, one word, responsive, unison, etc. But it is common for people to pray out loud during the service.

5. Following the Moravian principle, "no one ministers unless someone prays." When the worship team meets, they don't just do a quick prayer at the beginning of their worship time. For example, they read and pray through the words of a few songs they will be doing on Sunday. They take time to worship unrelated to Sunday. They pray for the upcoming worship experience, that people will enter into the flow of worship, etc. Or when planning a Vacation Bible School, leaders not only ask for people to coordinate the crafts, games, or stories, they also ask for a person to direct the prayer. And perhaps they have a team actually praying during the VBS itself. Hopefully each ministry team incorporates prayer into all it does.

6. There is an appreciation and application of "all kinds of prayers" (Eph. 6:18). Pray-ers are skilled in many types of prayers—intercession, worship-based prayer, prayer for specific requests, and so on. There is also an appreciation for many styles: quiet, loud, solo, all-together at the same time, and others.

7. At the leadership meetings they "pray as much as they discuss." This was a challenge given to me as a pastor—and our normal pattern for years. We tried to spend as much time in prayer during our meetings as we did discussing issues.

8. There is a "prayer" line in the budget and a specific person who manages it.

9. Any prayer pastor or coordinator (whatever term is used) is seen and recognized as staff, whether paid or volunteer.

10. Ephesians 6:18 does a great job of summarizing some key points here. Praying . . .

- in the Spirit—sensitive to specific things the Spirit wants us to pray about.

- on all occasions—large groups, small groups, individuals, home groups, etc.
- with all kinds of prayer—offering all our requests.
- while being alert—keeping the prayers fresh and letting the Spirit's creativity flow through our prayers.
- always keep on—the value is not seen only in the results, but in the process.
- for all the Lord's people—a variety of needs.

This one verse in Ephesians offers a great start on describing a culture of prayer!

Compiled by Prayer Connect

FROM INTENTIONAL TO INSTINCTIVE

I like comparing our approach to prayer to Beethoven's Fifth," said Dr. James Banks of Peace Church, Durham, NC. "We take the same theme and repeat it over and over again, with a slight modification."

In the preparation of this issue, we sent 30 pastors a questionnaire about developing a prayer culture in their churches. The churches are of varying sizes—from 50 members to 8,000 and everything in between. They are also in various stages of prayer growth. We found the data intriguing and helpful, and we hope it will both enlighten and challenge other pastors and church leaders.

What Does It Mean?

First, we asked pastors to describe a culture of prayer.

"A culture of prayer is a culture that does not just talk about prayer, but actually prays over events and decisions," said Paul Covert, prayer pastor at Central Christian Church, Mesa, AZ. He went on to say that a church with this culture "looks for ways to introduce prayer into every ministry of the church."

"Such a church," offered Nick Cardases, formerly pastor of Trinity Evangelical Missionary Church, Waterloo, Ontario, Canada, "would have everything born out of prayer, rather than prayer being one of the ministries."

Paul Bartnick of the Alliance Church of Zephyrhills, FL, wrote "Prayer is just as essential as preaching and teaching the Word. Prayer is just as essential as engaging in global missions."

"A [prayer] culture exists when a body is confronted with time constraints and the events [it] chooses to cut are not the prayer events. Then the church truly believes that prayer is [its] lifeline and connection to the Triune God," said Scott Roberts of Hope in Christ Church, Bellingham, WA.

David Chotka, lead pastor of Spruce Grove Alliance Church, in Spruce Grove, Alberta, Canada, stated that "each ministry, each outreach, each mission, each worship service, and each leader has praying leaders, praying ministries—and each major area of endeavor has a clearly identified prayer team. Prayer is a significant factor in board governance and staff meetings, and each pastor [on staff] is required to have a structured daily prayer life."

"A 'culture' in a congregation is a lived-out core value," responded Vince McFarland of Maryland Community Church, Terre Haute, IN. "Not just a value of words, but a value of the way things are done. Prayer is a 'first-nature' quality of living and the power behind decision making. Worship gatherings are 'filled with prayer.'"

Sunder Krishnan of Rexdale Alliance Church in Toronto, Ontario, Canada, said, "There is a pervasive sense and awareness throughout the congregation of the fundamental importance of prayer, both individually and corporately." The people in such a congregation, added Krishnan, "are not surprised when the leadership regularly issues calls for corporate gatherings of prayer for a variety of reasons, as well as a consistent encouragement to the pursuit of [a] personal life of intimacy and prayer."

Pastor Jeff Noel of Grace Heartland Church, Elizabethtown, KY, noted that "the culture or DNA is simply what the church does without thinking about it. It moves from intentional to instinctive. The first Church didn't 'think' about praying, they just prayed. Unfortunately that is not the culture of most churches in [the Western world]." Noel went on to say, "We had to intentionally begin the process of making prayer a priority through many different prayer activities. But over the past five years we have experienced those intentional actions become part of the natural culture of how we do church. It is now our DNA. Without prayer we would not be the same church, and people would sense the difference."

As these pastors shared, several similarities emerged. A culture of prayer does not just happen. Pastor Noel's church is not alone in being purposeful; churches need to take very intentional steps to make prayer a priority. Another similarity that emerged is how "in your face" these churches are becoming in regard to prayer, both with creative prayer activities and in what they require in prayer participation—especially of their elders and staff teams.

Becoming Intentional

Many of our pastors believe that for people to understand how important prayer is to their church, there needs to be a balance between making sure prayer is visible and developing prayer behind the scenes.

"What people see is what they unconsciously think matters," said Roberts. "But if the only prayers that occur in the life of a body are the 'visible' ones, then prayer isn't undergirding everything. The church must have a life of prayer that extends beyond the visible into every nook and cranny of the body's life."

"[Prayer] shouldn't be just a show," said Pastor Mike Sager of Faith Church, Austin, MN. "The distinction or earmark of authenticity is that it stems from personal healthy prayer lives, and is not just seen as an activity one does at church."

To assure that prayer grows in the lives of people, most of our represented churches are taking aggressive steps to disciple people in their prayer lives. They also require participation of their leaders.

"If leaders are not in sync about prayer," said Sager, "then we keep plodding and praying until they are. If leaders don't have a common conviction and practice about prayer's priority, then a culture of prayer cannot be developed."

Dee Duke of Jefferson Baptist in Jefferson, OR, indicated that leaders are "asked to write their personal and ministry goals for the year and to include their prayer goals. These would be their involvement in corporate prayer, private prayer, and [prayer] with their wife and family." Then there is accountability, said Duke. At most leader meetings time is spent talking about how they are doing with those goals.

Pastor Chotka said that he personally interviews potential elders and staff about their prayer lives. "How do you hear the Lord's voice?" is one of the questions he always asks. "[My] staff will be prayerful or they won't work with me," said Chotka. He regularly carves out time to go into each staff person's office to spend an hour of prayer with him or her. Their elders always pray for at least an hour before moving into any kind of organizational discussion.

Bartnick echoed what a number of these pastors said: "If they [leaders] refuse to learn and develop a prayer life, they disqualify themselves from leadership and need to be replaced."

Not only are these praying churches intentional about what they expect from the leaders regarding prayer, they are very intentional about placing prayer in front of their people. "I once read that vision is lost in 30 days," said Pastor Tom Swank of Northpoint Community Church, Fort Wayne, IN. "If prayer is not visible, its role will soon be lost."

Several pastors have encouraged staff and elders to be deliberate about visible prayer. Cory Stout, who pastors Community Heights Alliance Church in Newton, IA, encourages his staff (nine individuals) to do "hallway" prayer each week.

"The idea is," said Stout, "that as we encounter people in conversations [each week at church], we don't just say 'I'll pray for you' and then walk away (and probably forget to pray for them); but rather that we take the time right then and there to say, 'Can I pray for you/with you about that?'" Each week at staff meeting Stout has everyone tell whom they prayed for.

I [Jonathan Graf] personally witnessed this when I spoke at Community Heights a few years ago. As I sat waiting for each Sunday morning service to begin, I was truly amazed by how many clusters of people I saw praying for one another in the sanctuary and lobby. People catch on when they see it modeled!

Stout went on to say, "Prayer must be emphasized, validated, and prioritized, whether that is on a Sunday morning in front of hundreds or in a small group in front of eight." But, Stout added, "I believe commitment, more so than visibility, is the highest goal."

That commitment to prayer is worked on heavily by Concord First Assembly in Concord, NC.

Associate Pastor Phil Bennett wrote that they encourage people to practice daily Bible study and prayer through a plan they call Brave Christian. Each of the 800 or so participants learns to hear God speak through daily Bible reading and prayer time. They then journal what they hear from God and what their responses are. Next they ask for a deeper commitment—and a smaller number become "Watchmen," who commit to pray for the ministries of the church. Hundreds have signed up to take a slot on the weekly 168-hour, 24/7 prayer schedule.

Rexdale Alliance Church begins each year with a week of prayer that includes prayer gatherings every night. Out of that week comes greater prayer participation in other things. They host a monthly Sunday evening concert of prayer, and have a missions prayer emphasis every Sunday night in September. They also have multiple days of prayer for elders and offer three different corporate prayer meetings each week.

Pastor Lloyd Peters of Fort St. John's Alliance Church in British Columbia, Canada, said he leads in prayer every Sunday morning because it is important for people to see a pastor lead them into the throne room. But, he said, "I pray like I talk. It's very conversational most of the time." People need to see honest, everyday prayer to realize they can do it, too, Peters says.

Devoted to Prayer

National prayer leader Dennis Fuqua, who pastored a local church for more than 20 years and now heads up International Renewal Ministries (Pastors' Prayer Summits), reminded us that "devoted to prayer" is a description that was used seven times in the New Testament. The early Church did not view prayer as something to use only when it was in trouble or something used at the beginning and end of a service. Prayer was as important as the spoken Word, fellowship, or the breaking of bread (see Acts 2:42).

"Prayer is so much a part of what we do," said Dr. Banks, "that it permeates things, and the sense of God's presence soon follows."

"Culture of prayer is an attitude," commented

Stout. "An attitude of dependence. An attitude that says that we are incapable on our own—and thus reliant upon the person and power of Jesus Christ."

EDITOR'S NOTE: This article was compiled by Jonathan Graf, publisher of *Prayer Connect* and president of the Church Prayer Leaders Network. You can read complete responses to the questionnaire online at *prayerconnect.net/magazine/issue-10---upper-room/instinctive/pastors*.

Get a **GREATER** CONNECTION . . .

. . . and a **15%** DISCOUNT

Subscribe to **PRAYER**CONNECT

There are three types of annual subscriptions: Digital (online) $19.99, Print $24.99 and CPLN Membership (print plus more) $30. (All three give you digital access.) You can order them online at **www.prayershop.org.** Click on "Prayer Connect Magazine" and "Subscriptions." Use Code BKUR13 at checkout to receive a special 15% discount offered only to users of this booklet. Or fill out the form on the reverse side of this card and mail it with a check to *Prayer Connect*.

(Money Back Guarantee: If after receiving your first copy of *Prayer Connect*, you are not satisfied, you may request a refund within 60 days of your order and we will refund the full amount of your purchase. After 60 days we will refund the remaining amount of your subscription.)

www.**prayerconnect**.net

PRAYERCONNECT

To subscribe by mail, fill out this form, enclose a check made out to Prayer Connect and mail to:

PRAYERCONNECT
P.O. Box 10667
Terre Haute, IN 47801

CODED PRICES: Digital–$16.99; Print–$21.24; CPLN–$25.50

Name: _____

Address: _____

City: _____ ST: _____ Zip: _____

Email: _____

(Canadian and International subscribers must subscribe online with code. Your pricing on Print or CPLN is higher due to shipping costs.)

BKUR13